HANA'S SUITCASE

—A TRUE STORY—

KAREN LEVINE

D0273313

L940.
531

First published in this edition in 2012 by
Evans Brothers Ltd
2A Portman Mansions
Chiltern St
London W1U 6NR

www.evansbooks.co.uk

Published by permission of Second Story Press,
Toronto, Ontario, Canada

All rights reserved. No part of this publication may be reproduced,
stored in a retrieval system, or transmitted in any form or by any
means, electronic, mechanical photocopying, recording or otherwise,
without the prior permission of the Publisher.
Copyright © 2002 by Karen Levine

British Library Cataloguing in Publication Data
Levine, Karen
Hana's Suitcase
1. Brady, Hana - Juvenile literature 2. Holocaust, Jewish (1939-
1945) - Czech Republic - Juvenile literature 3. Jewish children -
Czech Republic - Biography - Juvenile literature
I. Title
940.5'318'092

Printed by Everbest Printing Company Ltd in Yau Tong Kowloon,
Hong Kong, September 2011, Job number (CAG1639)

ISBN 9780237545352

For my parents,
Helen and Gil Levine.

Introduction

Hana's Suitcase is a true story that takes place on three continents over a period of almost seventy years. It brings together the experiences of a girl and her family in Czechoslovakia in the 1930s and 40s, a young woman and a group of children in Tokyo, Japan and a man in Toronto, Canada in modern times.

Between 1939 and 1945, the world was at war. Nazi dictator Adolf Hitler wanted Germany to rule the world. At the centre of his vision was the brutal elimination of the Jewish people from the face of the earth. To get rid of his 'enemies', he set up dozens of prison camps called concentration camps across Europe. Jewish women, men and children from almost every country on the continent were deported; they were torn from their homes and sent to the camps, where they endured terrible suffering. Many people died of hunger and disease. Most were murdered. In these death camps and elsewhere where Hitler's followers carried out his terrible plan, six million Jews were killed. One-and-a-half million Jewish children were among them.

In 1945, the war ended and the entire world learned the horrors of what had gone on in the concentration camps. Since then, people have been trying to understand more about what is today known as the 'Holocaust', the worst example of mass murder or genocide in human history. How did it happen? How can we make sure it will never happen again?

In Japan, a country allied with Nazi Germany during the Second World War, attention to the history of the Holocaust is relatively new. An anonymous Japanese donor, who wanted to contribute to global tolerance and understanding, decided it was important for young people in Japan to learn more about this aspect of world history. Single-handedly, this donor has endowed the Tokyo Holocaust Education Resource Centre, which is dedicated to that purpose.

At a Children's Forum on the Holocaust held in 1999, two hundred pupils from schools in the Tokyo area met Holocaust survivor Yaffa Eliach. She told them about how almost every Jew in her village, young and old, was murdered by the Nazis. At the end of her talk, she reminded her audience that children have the power 'to create peace in the future'. A dozen of the young Japanese people there took her challenge to heart and formed a group called 'Small Wings'. Now the members of Small Wings, aged eight to eighteen, meet every month. They publish a newsletter, help run the Tokyo Holocaust Education Resource Centre and work to interest other Japanese children in the history of the Holocaust. They do their work under the guidance of Fumiko Ishioka, the director of the Tokyo

Holocaust Centre.

The suitcase — Hana's suitcase — is a key to the success of their mission. In it lies a story of terrible sadness and great joy, a reminder of the brutality of the past and of hope for the future.

HANA'S SUITCASE

Tokyo, Japan,
Winter 2000

Really, it's a very ordinary looking suitcase. A little tattered around the edges, but in good condition.

It's brown. It's big. You could fit quite a lot in it — clothes for a long trip, maybe. Books, games, treasures, toys. But there is nothing inside it now.

Every day children come to a little museum in Tokyo, Japan to see this suitcase. It sits in a glass cabinet. And through the glass you can see that there is writing on the suitcase. In white paint, across the front, there is a girl's name: Hana Brady. A date of birth: 16 May, 1931. And one other word: *Waisenkind*. That's the German word for orphan.

The Japanese children know that the suitcase came from Auschwitz, a concentration camp where millions of people suffered and died during the Second World War between 1939 and 1945. But who was Hana Brady? Where did she come from? Where was she travelling to? What did she pack? How did she become an orphan? What kind of girl was she and what happened to her?

The children are full of questions. So is the director of the museum, a slender young woman with long black hair named Fumiko Ishioka.

Fumiko and the children gently take the suitcase out of the glass case and open it. They search the side pockets. Maybe Hana left something that would be a clue. Nothing. They look under the polka-dot lining. There are no hints there either.

Fumiko promises the children to do everything she can to find out about the girl who owned the suitcase, to solve the mystery. And for the next year, she becomes a detective, scouring the world for clues to the story of Hana Brady.

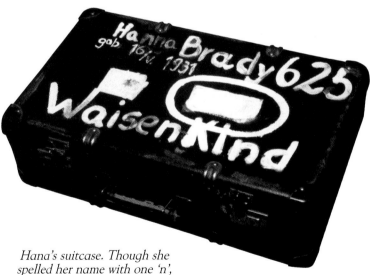

Hana's suitcase. Though she spelled her name with one 'n', the German spelling has two, as on the suitcase.

The town of Nove Mesto and its surroundings.

Nove Mesto, Czechoslovakia, 1930s

In rolling hills in the middle of what was then Czechoslovakia, in a province called Moravia, there was a town called Nove Mesto. It wasn't big, but it was famous. And in the winter, especially, it was a very busy place. People from all over the country came to cross-country ski in Nove Mesto. There were races to be raced. There were trails to be blazed and there were frozen ponds for skating. In the summer, there was swimming, sailing, fishing and camping.

Nove Mesto was home to 4,000 people. Once the town was well known for making glass. But in the 1930s, people worked in the forests and in little work-shops that made skis. On the main street, there was a large, two-storey white building. It had a two-storey attic. And in its basement, a secret passageway led to a church on the town's main square. In olden days, when the town was under siege, it was used by soldiers to store food and supplies for the people of Nove Mesto.

The town's shop was on the ground floor. There, you could buy almost anything: buttons, jam, oil lamps and rakes, sleigh bells, stones for sharpening knives, dishes, paper and pens and sweets. On the second floor lived the Brady family: father Karel, mother Marketa, Hana and her big brother George.

Father worked six days a week in the store. He was an athlete, known to almost everyone in Nove Mesto for his love of football, skiing and gymnastics. He was also an amateur actor with a big booming voice that could be heard from one end of a playing field to the other. Because of this, Father was chosen to commentate on the cross-country ski races over a megaphone, so that everyone could hear the action. He was a volunteer firefighter who, with other men from the town, drove the fire engine to help people in emergencies.

The Brady family opened their home to artists of all kinds — musicians, painters and poets, sculptors and actors. When they were hungry, they could always find a hot meal, produced by Boshka, the family cook. And their artistic talents found an eager audience, which, of course, included two impish children — Hana and George. Sometimes George was called upon to play his violin. Hana was more than willing to demonstrate her skill on the piano to anyone who would listen. And in the middle of the living room, there was a record player that was wound up by hand. Hana played her favourite song — 'I Have Nine Canaries' — over and over again.

Hana in costume for a school play.

Mother was a warm and generous hostess with a good sense of humour and a very loud laugh. She, too, worked six days a week in the shop and people often came in just to hear her jokes and banter. She paid special attention to poor people in Nove Mesto who lived on the outskirts of town. Once a week, she would prepare a bundle of food and clothing that Hana would deliver to needy neighbours. Hana was very proud of her mission and she nagged her mother to make care packages more often.

Hana was a helper in the store, too. From the time they were very small, Hana and George had the job of keeping the shelves stocked, clean and tidy. They learned how to slice yeast, chisel small lumps off the sugar loaf, weigh spices and seasonings, and twist paper into the shape of hollow cones to be filled with sweets

Nove Mesto. The Brady family lived on the second floor of the fourth building from the left. Their shop was on the ground floor.

and sold as treats. Once in a while, Mother noticed that some of those sweets cones were missing. Hana never told on George. And he never told on Hana.

There were always cats around the store, who worked full-time as mouse catchers. But once, as a special treat, Mother and Father ordered fluffy white angora kittens as pets for the children. Two soft little bundles arrived through the post in a box with breathing holes. At first, Sylva, the family wolfhound, a huge grey furry creature, sniffed around them suspiciously. But soon the kittens, who Hana named Micki and Mourek, became members of the family.

Hana and George went to the local school. They were ordinary children, who got into the usual mischief and had the usual problems and triumphs. There was just one thing that was different about them.

The Bradys were Jewish. They weren't a religious family. But Mother and Father wanted the children to know about their heritage. Once a week, while their playmates were at church, Hana and George sat with a special teacher who taught them about Jewish holidays and Jewish history.

There were a few other Jewish families in Nove Mesto. But Hana and George were the only Jewish children in the town. In their early years no one really noticed or cared that they were different. Soon, though, the fact that they were Jews would become the most important thing about them.

Tokyo,
Winter 2000

Back in her office, half a world away in Japan and more than half a century later, Fumiko Ishioka remembered how the suitcase had come to her.

In 1998, she had begun her job as coordinator of a small museum, called the Tokyo Holocaust Centre. It was dedicated to teaching Japanese children about the Holocaust. At a conference in Israel, Fumiko had met a few Holocaust survivors, people who had lived through the horrors of the concentration camps. She was astonished by their optimism and their joy in life,

The Holocaust Education Resource Centre in Tokyo, Japan.

Fumiko teaching children at the Centre about the Holocaust.

despite everything they had been through. When Fumiko felt sad about things in her own life, she often thought about these survivors. They were so strong-willed and wise. They had so much to teach her.

Fumiko wanted young people in Japan to learn from the Holocaust as well. It was her job to make it happen. And it wasn't an easy one. How, she wondered, could she help Japanese children understand the terrible story of what happened to millions of Jewish children on a faraway continent over fifty years ago?

She decided the best way to start would be through physical objects that the children could see and touch. She wrote to Jewish and Holocaust museums all over the world — in Poland, Germany, the United States and Israel — asking to borrow artifacts that had belonged to children. She posted her

11

request on the Internet. She wrote to individuals she thought might be able to help. Fumiko was looking for a pair of shoes and for a suitcase.

Everyone turned her down, telling her that the objects they had so carefully preserved were too precious to send to such a small museum, so far away. Fumiko wasn't sure what to do next. But she wasn't the kind of person who gave up easily. Just the opposite. The more rejections she got, the more dedicated she became.

That autumn, Fumiko travelled to Poland where many Nazi concentration camps had been located. There, on the site of the most well-known camp, she visited the Auschwitz Museum. Fumiko begged for a short meeting with the Museum's assistant director. She was given five minutes to explain what she wanted. When she left the assistant director's office, she had a promise that her request would be considered.

A few months later, a package from the Auschwitz Museum arrived. It contained a child's sock and shoe, a child's jumper, a can of Zyklon B poisonous gas and one suitcase — Hana's suitcase.

Fumiko Ishioka and one of the children visiting the Education Resource Centre.

Hana loved to play outdoors when she was young.

Nove Mesto, 1938

Hana had blonde hair, blue eyes and a very pretty round face. She was a strong girl. Once in a while, Hana would start a fight with George, just to show off her muscles. Even though her brother was three years older, Hana would sometimes emerge the winner. But most of the time, Hana and George played well together.

In the summer, in the stream behind their house, they pretended to be in the navy. Climbing into an old wooden bathtub, the children sailed along until one or the other pulled the plug in the middle and they sank, laughing and splashing. There were three different kinds of swings in the meadow at the back of the house — one for a small child, a two-seater, and one that swung from a giant tree out over the stream. Sometimes, the neighbourhood children would gather there for swinging contests. Who could swing the highest? Who could jump the farthest? Often it was Hana.

In the long halls of their apartment over the store, Hana raced on her red scooter, George on his blue one. In the winter, Hana and George built snow forts and skied. But Hana's greatest love was skating, and she worked hard perfecting her pirouettes on Nove Mesto's frozen pond. Sometimes, when she wore her special red

Above: The children building a snow fort.

Left: Hana in her special red skating outfit.

skating outfit — the one with the white fur on the ends of the sleeves — she imagined herself a dancing princess. Her parents, her friends and her brother applauded both the performance and the dream.

Because her parents worked six days a week, Sunday mornings were special for the family. When they woke up, George and Hana would snuggle up in their parents' bed under the fluffy feather eiderdown. On Sunday afternoons in the summer, they would all pile into the car and head off to the nearest fort or castle for a picnic, sometimes with Uncle Ludvik and Aunt Hedda who also lived in Nove Mesto. In the winter, there were sleigh rides and long cross-country skiing adventures. Hana was a very strong skier. On the eight-kilometre run between Nove Mesto and a nearby village (which had a wonderful tearoom with delicious creamy pastries), Hana always led the big family pack of cousins, even though she was the youngest.

But by New Year's Eve 1938, there was a new and menacing feeling in the air. There was talk of war. Adolf Hitler and his Nazis were in power in Germany. Earlier that year, Hitler had taken over Austria. Then he had marched his armies into parts of Czechoslovakia. Refugees — people trying to escape the Nazis — started appearing at the Bradys' door, asking for money, food and shelter. They always found a warm welcome from Mother and Father. But the children were mystified. Who are these people? Hana wondered. Why are they coming here? Why don't they want to stay in their own homes?

In the evenings, after Hana and George had been sent to bed, Mother and Father would sit by the radio and listen to the news. Often friends came and joined them, and they would talk long into the night about the news they had heard. "We'll keep our voices down," they would say, "so as not to wake the children."

The conversation of the adults was so intense, the discussions so heated, that they rarely heard the squeak of floorboards in the darkened hall, as Hana and George tiptoed to their secret listening post just outside the living room. The children heard the talk about the new anti-Jewish laws in Austria. They heard about *Kristallnacht* in Germany, when gangs of Nazi thugs roamed through Jewish neighbourhoods, breaking windows in homes and shops, burning synagogues, and beating people in the streets.

"It couldn't happen here, could it?" Hana whispered to her brother.

"Shhhh," said George. "If we talk now, they'll hear us and we'll be sent back to bed."

One night, their neighbour Mr. Rott presented a shocking idea to the adults. "We can all feel that a war is coming," he began. "It's not safe for Jews to be here. We should all leave Nove Mesto, leave Czechoslovakia, for America, for Palestine, for

Both Hana and George learned to ski when they were very young.

Canada. For anywhere. Leave now, before it's too late."

The rest of the group was taken aback. "Are you crazy, Mr. Rott?" one asked. "This is our home. This is where we belong." And that settled that.

Despite the bad times, the Bradys were determined to celebrate the coming of 1939. On New Year's Eve, after a feast of turkey, sausage, salami and pudding, the children got ready to play the traditional game of predicting the future. Hana, George and their young cousins from nearby towns were given half a walnut into which they each wedged a small candle. A large basin of water was dragged into the middle of the room. Each child launched a little walnut boat into it. Eleven-year-old George's boat wobbled in the water, turned round and round, and finally came to a stop, lopsided. His candle kept burning. Eight-year-old Hana launched hers and, for a moment, it glided along without a quiver. Then it shook, turned on its side, and the candle hit the water and went out.

Tokyo,
March 2000

From the day the suitcase arrived in Tokyo, Fumiko and the children were drawn to it. Ten-year-old Akira, who usually loved to joke and tease, wondered aloud what it would be like to be an orphan. Maiko, who was older, loved parties and was an accomplished synchronised swimmer. She always became very quiet in the presence of the suitcase. It made her think about being sent away from her own friends.

The suitcase was the only object they had at the Centre that was linked to a name. From the date on the suitcase, Fumiko and the children guessed that Hana would have been thirteen years old when she was sent to Auschwitz. A year younger than me, said one girl. Just as old as my big sister, said Akira.

Fumiko wrote back to the Auschwitz Museum. Could they help her find out anything about the girl who owned the suitcase? No, they replied. They knew no more than she did. Fumiko reported back to the children. "Try somewhere else," Maiko urged. "Don't give up," said Akira. The kids chanted encouragement like a chorus: "Keep on looking". Fumiko promised to do just that.

Fumiko wrote to Yad Vashem, Israel's Holocaust museum. No, we have never heard of a girl named Hana Brady, the director wrote. Have you tried the Holocaust Memorial Museum in Washington, DC? Fumiko rushed a letter off to Washington, but the reply was the same. We have no information about a girl named Hana Brady. How discouraging it was!

Then, out of the blue, Fumiko received a note from the museum at Auschwitz. They had discovered something. They had found Hana's name on a list. It showed that Hana had come to Auschwitz from a place called Theresienstadt.

Nove Mesto, 1939

On 15 March, 1939, Hitler's Nazi troops marched into the rest of Czechoslovakia and the Brady family's life was changed forever. The Nazis declared that Jews were evil, a bad influence, dangerous. From now on, the Brady family and the other Jews in Nove Mesto would have to live by different rules.

Jews could only leave their houses at certain hours of the day. They could only shop in certain shops and only at certain times. Jews weren't allowed to travel, so there were no more visits to beloved aunts, uncles, and grandmothers in nearby towns. The Bradys were forced to tell the Nazis about everything they owned — art, jewellery, cutlery, bank books. They hurriedly stashed their most precious papers under the floorboards in the attic. Father's stamp collection and Mother's silver were hidden with Gentile, non-Jewish friends. But the family radio had to be taken to a central office and surrendered to a Nazi official.

One day, Hana and George queued up at the cinema to see 'Snow White and the Seven Dwarfs'. When they got to the ticket booth they saw a sign that

Hana and George stood by each other as the Nazi restrictions increased.

read 'No Jews Allowed'. Their faces red, their eyes burning, Hana and George turned on their heels and headed for home. When Hana walked in the door, she was furious and very upset. "What is happening to us? Why can't I go to the cinema? Why can't I just ignore the sign?" Mother and Father looked grimly at each other. There were no easy answers.

Every week seemed to bring a new restriction. No Jews in the playground. No Jews on the sports fields. No Jews in the parks. Soon Hana could no longer go to the gym. Even the skating pond was declared off limits. Her friends — all of them Gentiles — at first were as mystified by the rules as Hana. They sat together in school as they always had, and still had good times making mischief in the classroom and in private gardens. "We'll be together forever, no matter what," promised Hana's best friend Maria. "We're not going to let anyone tell us who we can play with!"

But gradually, as the months dragged on, all Hana's playmates, even Maria, stopped coming over after school and at the weekends. Maria's parents had ordered her to stay away from Hana. They were afraid the Nazis would punish their whole family for allowing Maria to be friends with a Jewish child. Hana was terribly lonely.

With each loss of friendship and with each new restriction, Hana and George felt their world grow a little smaller. They were angry. They were sad. And they were frustrated. "What can we do?" they asked their parents. "Where can we go now?"

Mother and Father tried their best to distract the children, to help them find new ways to have fun. "We are lucky," Mother told them, "because we have such a big garden. You can play hide-and-seek. You can swing from the trees. You can invent games. You can play detective in the storerooms. You can explore the secret tunnel. You can play charades. Be grateful that you have each other!"

Hana and George were grateful to have each other and they did play together, but it didn't make them feel any better about all the things they couldn't

Hana and her mother hanging out the washing.

do anymore, all the places they couldn't go. On a fine spring day, when the sun was shining, the two of them sat in the meadow, bored, fiddling with the grass. Suddenly Hana burst into tears. "It's not fair," she cried. "I hate this. I want it to be like it was before." She yanked a fistful of grass out of the ground and threw it in the air. She looked at her brother. She knew he was as miserable as she was. "Wait here," he said. "I have an idea." In minutes he was back, carrying a pad of paper, a pen, an empty bottle and a shovel.

"What's all that for?" Hana asked.

"Maybe if we write down all the things that are bothering us," he said, "it'll help us feel better."

"That's stupid," Hana replied. "It won't bring back the park or the playground. It won't bring back Maria."

But George insisted. He was, after all, the big brother, and Hana didn't have a better idea. And so for the next few hours, the children poured their unhappiness onto paper, with George doing most of the writing and Hana doing much of the talking. They made lists of things they missed, lists of things they were angry about. Then they made lists of all the things they would do, all the things they would have and all the places they would go when these dark times were over.

When they were done, George took the sheets of paper, rolled them into a tube, stuffed them into the bottle and popped in the cork. Then the two of them walked back towards the house, stopping at the double swing. There, Hana dug a big hole. This would be a hiding place for some of their sadness and frustration. George placed the bottle at the bottom of the hole and Hana filled the space back up with earth. And when it was all over the world seemed a little lighter and brighter, at least for the day.

It was hard to make sense of everything that was happening. Especially now that the family radio was gone. Father and Mother had depended on hearing the eight o'clock news every night from London to keep them informed of Hitler's latest evil act. But Jews had been ordered to be inside their houses by eight. Listening to the radio was absolutely forbidden and the penalty for breaking any law was very severe. Everyone was afraid of being arrested.

Father hatched a plan, an ingenious way to get around the Nazi rules. He asked his old friend, the keeper of the big church clock, to do him a favour. Would he mind, Father asked, turning the clock back fifteen minutes in the early evenings? That way Father could rush to the neighbour's house, hear the news, and be safely home when the bell rang at eight (which was actually eight-fifteen). The Nazi guard who patrolled the town square didn't have a clue. And Father was thrilled that his scheme had worked. Unfortunately, the news he was able to hear on the radio was bad. Very bad. The Nazis were winning every battle, advancing on every front.

Hana and George.

Tokyo, March 2000

Theresienstadt. Now Fumiko and the children knew that Hana had come to Auschwitz from Theresienstadt. Fumiko was excited. This was the first solid piece of information she had found about Hana. The first clue.

Theresienstadt was the name that the Nazis gave to the Czech town of Terezin. It was a pretty little town, with two imposing fortresses, first built in the 1800s to hold military and political prisoners. After the Nazis invaded Czechoslovakia, they turned Terezin into the Theresienstadt ghetto — a walled, guarded, over-crowded prison town to hold Jews who had been forced to leave their homes. Over the course of World War Two, more than 140,000 Jews were sent here — 15,000 of them were children.

Fumiko stayed up late at night, her office a glow of light in the darkened Centre, reading everything she could find about Theresienstadt.

She learned that terrible things had happened in Theresienstadt, and that over the course of a few years almost everyone in the ghetto was deported again, put on trains and sent off to the more terrible concentration camps in the east which were known to be death camps.

But Fumiko also learned that brave and inspiring things happened in Theresienstadt. Among the adults were some very special people — great artists, famous musicians, historians, philosophers, fashion designers, social workers. They were all in Theresienstadt because they were Jews. An astonishing amount of talent, training and knowledge was crowded inside the walls of the ghetto. Under the noses of the Nazis and at great risk, the inmates secretly plotted and established an elaborate schedule of teaching, learning, producing and performing for both adults and children. They were determined to remind their students that — despite the war, despite the drab, cramped surroundings, despite everything — the world was a place of beauty and every individual person could add to it.

Fumiko also discovered that children in Theresienstadt were taught to paint and draw. And that, miraculously, 4,500 drawings created by these children had survived the war. Fumiko's heart began to beat more quickly. Could it be that among those drawings there might be one or more by Hana Brady?

Nove Mesto, Autumn 1940– Spring 1941

Autumn brought with it a chill in the air, as well as more restrictions, and hardship.

Hana was about to begin a new school year, when the Nazis announced that Jewish children would no longer be allowed to go to school. "Now, I will never see my friends!" Hana wailed, when her parents told her the bad news. "Now, I'll never become a teacher when I grow up!" She always dreamed of standing up at the front of the classroom and having everyone listen carefully to whatever she had to say.

Mother and Father were determined that both Hana and her brother would continue their education. Luckily, they had enough money to hire a young woman from the next village to be Hana's tutor, and an old refugee professor to teach George.

Mother tried to be cheerful. "Good morning, Hana," she would sing out when the sun rose. "It's time for breakfast. You don't want to be late for 'school'." Every morning, Hana would meet her new tutor at the dining room table. She was a kind young woman and she did her best to encourage Hana with reading, writing and arithmetic. She brought a small blackboard that she leaned up against a chair. Once in a while, she allowed Hana to draw with the chalk and bang out chalk dust from the board duster. But at this school, there were no playmates, no practical jokes, no playtime. Hana found it harder to pay attention or stay focused on her lessons. In the darkness of the winter, the world seemed to be closing in on the Brady family.

Indeed, when spring came, disaster struck. In March 1941, Mother was arrested by the Gestapo, Hitler's feared secret state police.

A letter came to the house ordering Mother to appear at nine o'clock in the morning at Gestapo headquarters in the nearby town of Iglau. In order to be there on time, she would have to leave in the middle of the night. She had one day to organise everything and say goodbye to her family.

She called Hana and George into the living room, sat on the couch, and pulled the children close to her. She told them that she would be going away for a while. Hana snuggled a little closer. "You must be good while I am gone," she said. "Listen carefully to Father and obey him. I will write," she promised. "Will you write back to me?"

George looked away. Hana trembled. The children were too shocked to reply. Their mother had never left them before.

Hana, her mother and George in happier times.

When Mother tucked Hana into bed that night, she held her tightly. Mother ran her soothing fingers through Hana's hair, just the way she had when Hana was very little. She sang Hana's favourite lullaby, over and over again. Hana fell asleep with her arms around her mother's neck. In the morning when Hana woke up, Mother was gone.

Tokyo,
April 2000

Fumiko could hardly believe it when a flat package arrived at her office in Tokyo. Just a few weeks earlier, she had written to the Terezin Ghetto Museum in what is now called the Czech Republic. Fumiko had explained in her letter how anxious she and the children were to find anything that would connect them more closely to Hana. People there said they knew nothing about Hana's personal story. But they did know about the huge collection of children's drawings

One of Hana's drawings from Theresienstadt.

that had been hidden in the camp. Many of the drawings were now displayed at the Jewish Museum in Prague.

Fumiko opened the package. She was so excited that her hands were shaking. There were photographs of five drawings. One was a coloured drawing of a garden and a park bench. Another showed people having a picnic beside a river. The rest were in pencil and charcoal, one of a tree, another of farmhands drying hay in a field, and another of stick people carrying suitcases, getting off a train. In the top right hand corner of each of the drawings was the name 'Hana Brady'.

Nove Mesto, Autumn 1941

Since she had made a promise to her mother, Hana did her best to behave well. She helped her father when she could and did her lessons. Boshka, their much-loved housekeeper, tried to cook Hana's favourite meals and give her extra helpings of dessert. But Hana missed her mother terribly, especially at night. No one else could smooth her hair with quite the same touch. No one else could sing her lullaby. And that big booming laugh of her mother's — everyone missed that.

The children learned that their mother was in a place called Ravensbruck, a women's concentration camp in Germany. "Is it far away?" Hana asked her father.

"When is she coming home?" George wanted to know. Father assured the children that he was doing everything he could to get her out.

One day Hana was reading in her room when she heard Boshka calling for her. She decided to ignore her. Hana didn't feel like doing any chores. And what else was there to look forward to? But Boshka kept calling. "Hana, Hana? Where are you? Come quickly! There is something very special waiting for you at the post office."

The gifts made from bread that Hana's mother sent to the family after she was taken away.

When she heard that, Hana dropped her book. Could it be what she hoped for most? She burst out of the house and ran down the street to the post office. Hana approached the counter. "Do you have something for me?" she asked. The woman behind the counter slid a small brown package through the hole. Hana's heart leapt when she recognised her mother's writing. Her fingers trembled as she opened it. Inside was a little brown heart. It was made of bread and had the initials 'HB' carved into it. Attached was a letter.

My dearest one, I wish you all the best on your birthday. I am sorry that I can't help you blow out the candles this year. But the heart is a charm I made for your bracelet. Are your clothes getting too small for you? Ask Daddy and Georgie to speak to your aunts about having some new ones made for my big girl. I think about you and your brother all the time. I am well. Are you being a good girl? Will you write me a letter? I hope you and George are keeping up your studies. I am well. I miss you so much, dearest Hanichka. I am kissing you now.

Love, Mother. May 1941. Ravensbruck.

Hana closed her eyes and clutched the little brown bread heart. She tried to imagine that her mother was standing beside her.

That autumn brought another blow. One day Father arrived home carrying three squares of cloth. On each was a yellow star of David and in the middle of the star one word: "Jude" — Jew.

"Come children,"

Jews were ordered to wear yellow cloth stars whenever they went out in public.

said Father, as he took a pair of scissors from a kitchen drawer. "We need to cut out these stars and pin them on our coats. We must wear them whenever we leave the house."

"Why?" asked Hana. "People already know we are Jews."

"It's what we must do," replied Father. He looked so dejected, sad and tired that Hana and George didn't argue.

From that day on, Hana went outside less often. She would do almost anything to avoid wearing the yellow badge in public. She hated the star. It was so humiliating. It was so embarrassing. Wasn't it enough, the children wondered, that they'd lost their park, their pond, their school and their friends? But now, when they left the house, the star was pinned to their clothing.

One Jewish man in town was not willing to obey. He'd had enough of all the rules and restrictions. So on a late September day in 1941, he left his house feeling a little brazen. He did not cut out the star and pinned the entire square cloth to his coat. This tiny act of rebellion was immediately noticed by the Nazi officer in charge in Nove Mesto. He was furious. He declared that Nove Mesto must be made "judenfrei", free of Jews, immediately.

The very next morning, a big black car driven by a Nazi officer drew up in front of the Bradys' house.

Four frightened Jewish men were already huddled inside it. There was a knock on the door. Father opened it. Hana and George hung behind him. The Gestapo officer barked at Father to come out immediately. Hana and George couldn't believe their ears. They stood there, stunned, terrified and silent. Father hugged the children, implored them to be brave. And then he, too, was gone.

Tokyo,
Spring 2000

Fumiko was enchanted by Hana's drawings. She knew they would help children imagine better what kind of person Hana had been. It would be easier for them to put themselves in her shoes. Fumiko was right.

More than ever, the children who volunteered at the Centre focused their attention on Hana. Led by

Another of Hana's drawings from Theresienstadt.

Maiko, some of them formed a group with a mission to let others know about what they were learning. They called their club 'Small Wings'. Once a month, they met to plan their newsletter. Everyone had a role. The older children wrote articles. The youngest were encouraged to draw pictures. Others wrote poems. With Fumiko's help, they sent their newsletter to schools far and wide, so others could find out about the history of the Holocaust and the search for Hana.

More than anything, they wanted to know what Hana looked like. They wanted to see the face of this little girl whose story they yearned to know. Fumiko realised that if she could find a photograph of Hana,

The Small Wings.

she would be even more alive to the children as a real human being. Fumiko was determined that the search would continue.

Now that she had the drawings, a sock, the shoe, the jumper, and, of course, Hana's suitcase, Fumiko felt it was time to open the exhibit she had been working towards, 'The Holocaust Seen Through Children's Eyes'.

Nove Mesto, Winter 1941–1942

Now there were only two children. No parents. George put an arm around his ten-year-old sister and promised to take care of her. Boshka, the housekeeper, tried to distract them with special treats and lighthearted talk. It didn't work. The children were sad and they were very scared.

Hours after their father's arrest there was another knock at the door. Hana's heart pounded. George swallowed hard. Who have they come for now? But when the children opened the door, they found Uncle Ludvik, their beloved Uncle Ludvik. "I've just heard the bad news," he said, hugging Hana with one arm, George with the other. "You are both coming with me. You belong with family, with people who love you."

Uncle Ludvik was a Christian who had married Father's sister. Because he wasn't Jewish, he was not an obvious target for the Nazis. But he was a brave man to take in George and Hana. The Gestapo had warned that terrible harm could come to anyone who helped the Jews.

Uncle Ludvik told the children to gather up their most treasured things. Hana took her life-sized doll

A younger Hana with George and her doll,
Nana, that was almost as big as Hana herself.

named Nana which she had had since she was five. George put together all the family photographs. Each of them filled a suitcase with clothes. Hana chose a large brown suitcase that she had taken before on family trips. She loved the polka-dot lining. When everything was packed, they turned out the light and closed the door behind them.

That night, her aunt and uncle tucked Hana into a big bed with a feather-filled eiderdown. "We will care for you until your parents come back, Hana," they promised. "And we'll be just down the hall, if you wake up in the night."

But long after lights out, Hana lay awake, blinking into the unfamiliar darkness. It was a strange bed. And the world — now full of danger — seemed to have turned upside down. What will come next? Hana wondered with fear. Finally, she closed her eyes and fell asleep.

Hana awoke the next morning to urgent barking outside her window. Her heart pounded. What could be wrong? Then she recognised the sounds. It was Sylva, their loyal wolfhound. She had found her way across town to be with Hana and George. At least some friends, Hana thought, stay true. It was a small comfort.

Aunt Hedda and Uncle Ludvik's house was small but comfortable, with a pretty little garden out the back. It was very close to the neighbourhood school,

Hana, George and their wolfhound, Sylva.

and every day George and Hana watched the other children with their book bags, laughing, playing, on their way to their classes. "I want to go too!" Hana stamped her foot in hurt and frustration. But there was nothing anyone could do.

In the months that followed, Uncle Ludvik and Aunt Hedda did their best to keep the children busy. George chopped wood for hours on end. Hana read books and played games. She was well liked by her cousins Vera and Jiri. Sometimes she even went to church with them.

Hana and her loving and brave Uncle Ludvik.

Hana and George helping out in the fields.

Later, at Theresienstadt, Hana drew this picture of people working in the fields.

And every day at lunchtime, Hana and George went back to their old home to eat a familiar meal with their housekeeper, Boshka, who pampered them, hugged and kissed them, and reminded them that she had promised their parents that she would keep them healthy by feeding them well.

Every few weeks a letter would arrive from Father, who was imprisoned in the Iglau Gestapo prison. George would read only the cheerful parts to his sister. George thought Hana was too young to know the whole truth about the harsh conditions in prison and how desperate Father was to be free. She was not too young, though, to be deported by the Nazis.

Nove Mesto, May 1942

One day, a notice was delivered to Aunt Hedda and Uncle Ludvik's house. Hana and George Brady were ordered to report to a deportation center at Trebic, fifty kilometres away from Nove Mesto, on 14 May, 1942. This was what Uncle Ludvik had feared. He called Hana and George into his study and read them the letter. Then he tried to put the bad news in the best possible light. "You're going on a trip," he told them. "Together! You'll be going to a place where there are lots of other Jews, lots of other children to play with. Maybe there you won't have to wear the star!" George and Hana said very little. They were both unhappy about being uprooted again and leaving their aunt and uncle.

Hana was scared. When Boshka came to help them prepare for this strange trip, Hana peppered her with questions. "Where are our parents? When will we see them again? Where will we end up? What can we take with us?" Boshka didn't have any answers. The housekeeper told Hana that she, too, would be leaving Nove Mesto to stay with a brother who lived on a farm.

Hana took out the large brown suitcase with the

JÜDISCHE KULTUSGEMEINDE IN PRAG
ŽIDOVSKÁ NÁBOŽENSKÁ OBEC V PRAZE

> Herrn, Frau, Fräulein
> Pan, paní, slečna
>
> *Brady Hanna*
>
> 100.436
>
> *Neustadtl Ms.*
>
> 13

Diese Vorladung ist mit Genehmigung der Zentralstelle für jüdische Auswanderung Prag (Dienststelle des Befehlshabers der Sicherheitspolizei beim Reichsprotektor in Böhmen und Mähren) als Reisegenehmigung anzusehen.	Tato obsílka platí za cestovní povolení na základě schválení Zentralstelle für jüdische Auswanderung Prag (Dienststelle des Befehlshabers der Sicherheitspolizei beim Reichsprotektor in Böhmen und Mähren).
Über Weisung der Zentralstelle für jüdische Auswanderung Prag haben Sie sich	Z nařízení Zentralstelle für jüdische Auswanderung Prag dostavíte se

am - dne **30. IV. 1942**

um - v **10**

in - do *Trebitsch* Uhr - hod.

einzufinden.

Jede vorgeladene Person hat mitzubringen: 1. Geburtschein, 2. Bürgerlegitimation (Kennkarte oder einen anderen Beleg über die Staatsbürgerschaft), 3. diese Vorladung. Neben diesen Personaldokumenten hat jede Person sämtliche Lebensmittelkarten mitzubringen.	Každá předvolaná osoba přinese s sebou 1. rodný list, 2. občanskou legitimaci (průkaz totožnosti nebo jiný úřední doklad o státní příslušnosti), 3. toto předvolání. Kromě těchto osobních dokladů, přinese každá osoba všechny potravinové lístky s sebou.

Um die vorgeschriebene Vorladungsstunde einhalten zu können, werden Sie den	Abyste dodržel(a) hodinu, na kterou jste byl(a) předvolán(a), použijete vlaku, který odjíždí

29.4.42 um - v **18'03**

von - : *Neustadtl n'ber Saar*

abgehenden Zug benützen.

Zur Rückreise müssen Sie, den

um - v **16'38** Uhr - hod.

vom Vorladungsort abgehenden Zug benützen. místo předvolání.

K návratu musíte nastoupiti do vlaku, který opouští

Kinder bis zu 4 Jahren müssen nicht persönlich erscheinen, doch müssen ihre Eltern oder verantwortl. Aufseher, sowohl die Personaldokumente, als auch diese Vorladung und die Lebensmittelkarte vorlegen. Kranke und alte Personen, die nicht persönlich erscheinen können, müssen neben allen Dokumenten ein amtsärztliches Zeugnis vorlegen lassen. Dieses Zeugnis muß eine genaue Diagnose der Krankheit enthalten.	Děti do 4 let se nemusí osobně dostaviti, avšak jejich rodiče nebo jejich zodpov. dozorce musí předložiti jak jejich osobní doklady, tak i toto předvolání a všechny potravinové lístky. Nemocné a staré osoby, které se nemohou osobně dostaviti, dají se sebe předložiti všechny doklady a mimo to vysvědčení úředního lékaře. Toto vysvědčení musí obsahovati přesnou diagnosu nemoci.

JÜDISCHE KULTUSGEMEINDE IN PRAG
ŽIDOVSKÁ NÁBOŽENSKÁ OBEC V PRAZE

This document orders Hana to be deported from her uncle's home on 30 April 1942. In fact, she was sent to Theresienstadt on 14 May.

polka-dot paper lining from under her bed. She packed a sleeping bag that she hoped would maintain the smell of home, no matter how far away they were sent. So did George. There was salami and sugar to tuck in amongst the clothes, as well as a few keepsakes.

Uncle Ludvik was heartbroken about sending his young niece and nephew away. He asked a driver to take them to the deportation centre. Uncle Ludvik just couldn't face it himself. He and his wife did their best to hide their tears as they said goodbye to Hana and George. They promised to wait for their return to Nove Mesto after the war was over. When the driver rang his bells, and the horses pulled away from the house, no one spoke a word.

A few hours later, the driver dropped Hana and George off in front of a huge warehouse. They joined the queue near the entrance. When they reached the registration desk, they gave their names to a frowning soldier. He waved them into the dark, airless building.

The floor inside the building was covered with mats. Hana and George found two mats together in a corner and sat down. When they looked around, they realised there were hardly any other children. But there were hundreds of Jewish men and women, waiting to be sent to a place called Theresienstadt. They were all being deported.

For four days and four nights, Hana and George stayed in the warehouse, eating the food from their suitcases, sleeping on the mats. Though some of the adults tried to be kind to the children, Hana and George were not in the mood for company. They had each other and they passed the time reading, talking, sleeping and thinking of home. It was in this warehouse on 16 May, 1942, with a few sweets and a stub of a candle, that Hana Brady celebrated her eleventh birthday.

Tokyo,
June 2000

The exhibition 'The Holocaust Seen Through Children's Eyes' drew more visitors, adults and children alike, than Fumiko had dreamed possible. The story of the Holocaust was new to many of the people who came to the Museum. As Fumiko had hoped, its tragedy was made real for them by the objects she had gathered and the story they told.

Though they were interested in the shoe, the can of Zyklon B gas, and the little jumper, it was the suitcase that became a magnet. Children and their parents constantly gathered around it and examined the writing: Hana Brady, 16 May, 1931, *Waisenkind* – orphan. They read the poems written by the members of Small Wings. And they admired the drawings Hana had made in Theresienstadt. "Do you know any more about her?" they asked. "What happened to her? What did she look like?" Fumiko decided to re-double her efforts to find a picture of Hana. Fumiko wrote back to the Terezin Ghetto Museum. No, came the answer. We already told you. We know nothing about a girl named Hana Brady.

Fumiko just couldn't accept this. She decided to go to Terezin herself.

Deportation Centre, May 1942

On the morning of the fourth day, a loud whistle blew, and a Nazi soldier marched into the warehouse. Hana and George huddled in their corner as he barked out the orders.

"Everyone is to appear at the train tracks in one hour. Each person is allowed one suitcase. Twenty-five kilos. Not a gram more. Form straight lines. No talking. Do as you are told."

The voice was so harsh, so scary. Hana and George quickly got their things together. Adults tried to help them, making sure the children were ready. Poor little ones, they thought. Such a hard journey and alone, with no parents.

Under the threatening eyes of the soldiers, they all left the warehouse in single file and lined up at the tracks. From the brilliant sunlight of the morning, Hana and George stepped into the dark train, carrying their suitcases. More people piled in after them, until it was full. Then the doors slammed shut and the train began to move.

Terezin, July 2000

Theresienstadt. The name the Nazis gave the Czech town of Terezin. Fumiko knew that to solve the mystery of Hana's suitcase, she had to get there. But how? The Czech Republic was thousands of miles from Japan and a plane ticket would cost a lot of money that Fumiko didn't have.

But this time luck was on her side. Fumiko was invited to attend a conference on the Holocaust in England. From there, it would only be a short plane trip to Prague, capital of the Czech Republic. From Prague it was just a two-hour drive to Terezin. Fumiko couldn't wait to leave.

On the morning of 11 July, 2000, Fumiko got off the bus in the main square of Terezin. At first glance, it looked like an ordinary pretty town. There were wide streets lined with trees and well-kept three-storey houses with flowered window boxes. But Fumiko hardly noticed. She had exactly one day to accomplish her mission. That night she would have to go back to Prague. Her plane for Japan was leaving the next morning.

Fumiko hadn't phoned ahead. She had no appointment at the Museum. But directly across the

Fumiko went to modern-day Terezin.

main square, she saw a long two-storey pale yellow building. This was the Terezin Ghetto Museum.

Fumiko opened the heavy front door and entered the cool foyer. It was eerily quiet. Where was everybody? She poked her head into a few of the offices off the main entranceway. They were empty. There seemed to be no one in the building.

What has happened? Fumiko wondered. Could it be that everyone is out at lunch? No, it's only ten o'clock in the morning. Fumiko went back out into the square and tapped the shoulder of a friendly looking man on a park bench. "Can you help me?" she asked. "I'm looking for someone to help me in the Museum."

"Oh, you won't find anyone there today, young lady. It's a holiday and all the people who work there are away celebrating," the man replied. "I'm afraid you're out of luck."

Theresienstadt, May 1942

The train trip was quiet, uneventful. People seemed to keep to themselves, lost in their own thoughts and fears about the future. After a few hours, the train came to an abrupt halt. The doors were flung open and the frightened passengers standing nearest to the doors could see the sign reading 'Bohusovic Station'. Hana squinted in the sunlight as she and George lugged their suitcases off the train. There, at the station, they were instructed to walk the rest of the way to the Theresienstadt fortress.

It was only a few kilometres, but their suitcases were cumbersome and heavy. Should we leave some things here, Hana and George wondered, to lighten our load? No, everything in their suitcases was precious, the only reminders of the life they used to have. George carried one suitcase. The other one they put on a moving cart, pushed by prisoners.

Hana and George approached the entrance to the walled fortress and joined a queue. Everyone was wearing a yellow star, just like them.

At the front of the line, a soldier asked people for their name, age and place of birth. Boys and men were

Hana drew this picture of people getting off a train while she was at Theresienstadt.

being sent in one direction, girls and women in another. "Where are they going?" Hana asked George. More than anything else, she was afraid of being separated from her brother. "Can I stay with you?" she pleaded.

"Be quiet, Hana!" George told his sister. "Don't make a fuss."

When they reached the front of the line, the soldier stared at them. "Where are your parents?" he demanded.

"They are, uh, in another, uh, camp," George stammered. "We hope that here we might be reunited."

The soldier wasn't interested in conversation. He wrote down their names on index cards and searched their suitcases for money and jewellery. Then he slammed the bags shut. "To the left!" he ordered

61

George. "To the right!" he ordered Hana.

"Please can I stay with my brother?" Hana asked.

"Move! Now!" the soldier ordered. What Hana feared most was about to happen. George gave her a quick hug. "Don't worry," he said. "I'll find you as soon as I can." Holding back tears, Hana picked up her suitcase and followed the other girls to *Kinderheim* (children's home) L410, a large barrack for girls that was to be Hana's home for the next two years.

Terezin,
July 2000

Fumiko couldn't believe it. She was very upset — with herself and with her bad luck. I've come all this way and everyone who might be able to help me is on holiday. How did I manage to pick such a bad time to come to the Terezin Museum? How could I be so stupid? she thought. What do I do now?

As the hot sun beat down on her, a tear of frustration rolled down Fumiko's cheek. She decided to go back inside the Museum to try and collect her thoughts. Maybe she could come up with a different plan.

As she sat on a bench in the foyer, she heard a rustling sound. It appeared to be coming from one of the offices at the end of the hall. Fumiko tiptoed in the direction of the sound. There, in the last office on the right, she found a woman with glasses perched on the end of her nose, sorting through a huge stack of papers.

Startled, the woman almost jumped out of her chair when she saw Fumiko. "Who are you?" she asked. "What are you doing here? The Museum is closed."

"My name is Fumiko Ishioka," she replied. "I have come a long way from Japan to find out about a little girl who was here in Theresienstadt. We have her suitcase in our museum in Tokyo."

"Come back another day," the woman replied politely, "and someone will try and help you."

"But I don't have another day!" exclaimed Fumiko. "My plane to Japan leaves tomorrow morning. Please," she pleaded. "Help me find Hana Brady."

The woman removed her glasses. She stared at the young Japanese woman and saw how anxious and determined she was. The Czech woman heaved a sigh. "All right," she said. "I can't promise anything. But I'll try and help you. My name is Ludmila."

Theresienstadt, 1942–43

Kinderheim L410 was a large plain building with about ten dormitory rooms. Twenty girls slept in each room, on burlap mattresses filled with straw in three-tiered bunk beds. Before the war, the town had been home to 5,000 people. The Nazis crammed ten times that number of prisoners into the same space.

There was never enough room, never enough food, never a chance for a private moment. There were too many people, too many bugs and rats, and too many Nazis who patrolled the camp with cruel discipline.

In the beginning, Hana, as a younger child, was not allowed to leave the building. That meant she couldn't see George. He lived in Kinderheim L417, which was just for boys, a few blocks away. Hana missed him terribly, and constantly asked the older girls, who were allowed outside, for news of him. They took Hana under their wing. They felt sorry for her, alone in the world, without her mother and father, away from her brother.

Hana made friends with an older girl in the next bunk. Ella was short, dark and very lively. She had a ready laugh and was happy to spend time with a younger girl who looked up to her and whom she could comfort in difficult times.

The man who gave out tickets for food took a liking to Hana and worried about her health. He knew that Hana was always hungry. He kindly offered to sneak her extra tickets for another ladle of watery soup, another hunk of black bread. Hana's stomach growled and her mouth watered at the prospect of more food. But each time the offer was made, she politely said no. She'd been warned by Ella and the other older girls that she would be in big trouble with the guards if she was caught breaking a rule.

Torn from their families, crammed into small spaces, with barely enough to eat, the girls set about trying to make the best of a very bad situation. The ones over fifteen worked in the garden, where fruits, vegetables and flowers were grown for the Nazi soldiers. Once in a while, Mr. Schwartzbart, who ran the garden, allowed Hana to come out with the working group and enjoy the fresh air and sun. Hana loved the chance to work in the garden with the older girls. And there was an added bonus. A green bean here, and a strawberry there always managed to find its way into a hungry girl's mouth.

But for the most part, Hana had to stay with girls her own age or younger, and obey the supervisor assigned to her room. Every day, they dusted, cleaned and swept under the bunks. Dishes, as well as faces, were washed under a pump. And every day there were secret classes held in the attic of Kinderheim L410.

In music classes, the girls learned new songs. They sang softly so they wouldn't be heard by the guards. At the end of each class, one child was chosen to sing a favourite song from home. When it was Hana's turn, she always sang a song called 'Stonozka', the centipede song.

> *Her life is not a piece of cake.*
> *Imagine how she suffers when*
> *She walks until her tootsies ache.*
> *She's got good reason to complain.*
> *So when I want to cry the blues*
> *I just recall the centipede.*
> *Consider walking in her shoes*
> *And then my life seems sweet indeed.*

There were sewing classes, too. Hana had never sewn a stitch in her life, and she had a hard time with the needle. The teacher often had to ask Hana to stop giggling when she made a silly mistake. Nonetheless she managed to finish a blue blouse of which she was very proud.

But Hana's favourite class was her art class. Painting and drawing supplies were hard to come by. Some people had smuggled them into the ghetto in

Hana's drawing of people having a picnic under an umbrella, beside a river.

suitcases. Paper had been stolen, sometimes at great risk, from the Nazi storerooms. Plain wrapping paper was used when nothing else could be found. One way or another, in the early days, there were always crayons and coloured pencils.

The art teacher, Friedl Dicker-Brandeis, had been a famous painter and was now a fellow prisoner at Theresienstadt. Friedl taught her pupils about serious things like perspective and texture. And sometimes the girls drew pictures of serious subjects: the ghetto walls, people waiting in line for food, inmates being beaten by Nazi soldiers.

But, more than anything, Friedl wanted her classes to help the children forget their brutal surroundings, at least for a while. "Think of space," she told Hana and the others. "Think of freedom. Let your imagination run wild. Tell me what is in your hearts. Put it down on paper."

For a treat, she would take them to the roof of the building, so they could be closer to the sky. From there, they could look beyond the walls of the camp and see the surrounding mountains in the distance. The girls could dream of birds and butterflies, of ponds and swings. And, using their crayons and pencils, they could bring them to life.

When classes were over and all the chores were done, they played a board game called *Smelina*, which had been invented right there in the ghetto. It was based on Monopoly, created for the children by an engineer named Oswald Pock who had been deported to Terezin. The players would land on properties like *Entwesung*, the de-lousing station where clothes were disinfected, and the guards' barracks. Instead of building a hotel, players built a *kumbal*, an attic hideaway above the barracks. For money, players used the ghetto paper bills called ghetto *kronen*.

But no matter what the distractions, Hana always ended up feeling hungry and lonely. She missed George terribly. Then one day there was an announcement that the ghetto rules were changing. The girls were allowed to go out once a week for two hours.

Hana immediately raced across the square to the Boys' House. "George, George Brady!" she called. "Where is my brother? Have you seen my brother?" She ran from room to room, asking every boy she came across. So anxious was Hana to find her brother that she even opened the door to a bathroom. And there was George, working away at his new job as a plumber. What a joyous reunion it was! George threw down his tools and Hana rushed into his arms. They laughed. They cried. Questions tumbled from their mouths. "Are you well? Have you heard anything about Mother and Father? Are you getting enough to eat?" From then on, they took advantage of every opportunity to be together.

George took his responsibility as a big brother seriously. He felt it was his job to protect Hana and to make sure she didn't get into trouble. He wanted to keep her as happy and healthy as possible until they could be with their parents again.

And Hana was equally devoted to George. In Terezin, where there was never enough to eat, residents received a small *buchta*, a plain doughnut, once a week. Hana never ate hers. She brought it to George so he could be strong and stay sweet.

In Theresienstadt, it seemed to Hana that more people arrived every day. Men, women and children came from all over Czechoslovakia at first, and then from other European countries. Every time a new group of people got off the trains, Hana would look for familiar faces. And sometimes, when she was feeling strong, she would approach strangers and ask, "Do you know my mother and father? Have you been to a place called Ravensbruck? My mother is there! Do you have any news of Karel and Marketa Brady?" The answer was always the same, but delivered with kindness and a barely concealed pity. "No dear, we don't know your mother and father. But if we hear anything — anything at all — we will find you and tell you."

Then one day, a familiar face did appear — an old friend of her parents who had no children of her own. At first, Hana was thrilled to see her. Anything that reminded Hana of home, that brought her a tiny step closer to her mother and father, was a comfort. But suddenly it seemed that wherever Hana went, the woman was waiting for her. Every time Hana turned a corner, she was there. She pinched Hana's cheek, gave her kisses. And then one day, she went too far.

"Come here, little one," she said, holding her hand out. "Remember all our good times together. Don't be shy. Don't be lonely. You can come and see me every day. You can call me 'mother'."

"I have a mother," Hana spat out. "Go away! Leave me alone." Hana refused to see the woman again. She missed her own mother. No one could take her place.

Terezin,
July 2000

At the Terezin Ghetto Museum, Ludmila sat down behind her desk and stared at the young Japanese woman perched on the edge of the seat across from her. Fumiko's determination was written all over her face. She liked Fumiko and wanted to help her find out more about this girl, this Hana Brady.

She pulled a big book off the shelves. Inside were the names of the almost 90,000 men, women and children who had been imprisoned at Theresienstadt and transported to the east. They turned to the B's: Brachova, Hermina. Brachova, Zusana. Brada, Tomas. Bradacova, Marta. Bradleova, Zdenka.

"Here she is," cried Ludmila. And there she was: Hana Brady, 16 May, 1931. "How can I find out more about her?" Fumiko asked.

"I wish I knew," Ludmila replied.

"But look," said Fumiko, pointing to another line in the book. There was another Brady, listed right above Hana. "Could this be her family?" Fumiko wondered aloud. Ludmila looked at the birth dates. Three years apart. "Yes," she said, "chances are very good that this was a brother. The Nazis listed families together."

..en ke studijním účelům
PAMÁTNÍK TEREZÍN
vzdělávací oddělení

581 Wolfenstein Helene	Haushalt	15. 6. 1890	Gr. Meseritsch Oberstadt 350	100716
582 Wolfenstein Walter	Arbeiter	19.10. 1913	Gr. Meseritsch Oberstadt 350	100719
583 Wolfenstein Sidonie	Schneiderin	10. 1. 1911	Gr. Meseritsch Oberstadt 350	100718
584 Schück Ing. Friedrich	Masch.Ing.	23. 6. 1891	Unter Dobrau 81	100646
585 Drechsler Simon	Kaufmann	3. 8. 1818	Gr. Meseritsch Jalimilg.56	100463
586 Schnabel Rudolfine	Haushalt	30. 3. 1877	Unter Dobrau 81	100643
587 Schück MUDr. Ottokar	Arzt	4.11. 1894	Unter Dobrau 81	100649
588 Schück Edith	Haushalt	17. 5. 1507	Unter Dobrau 81	100641
589 Schück Jagmar	Schülerin	30. 3. 1933	Unter Dobrau 81	100643
590 Schück Zdenko	Schüler	31. 7. 1938	Unter Dobrau 81	100650
591 Fein Anna	Private	9. 6. 1890	Neustadtl i.M.133	100491
592 Lauer Irma	Hausgehilfin	21. 8. 1911	Teltsch,Lindekgl81 dzt.Trebitsch Iglauer for 1	101107
593 Thierfeld Emma	Haushalt	13. 3. 1887	Stadt Saar 65	100636
594 Schwartz Irene 4.	Fotografin	3.13. 7.15	Stadt Saar 65	100654
595 Thierfeld Paul	Arbeiter	16. 3. 1935	Stadt Saar 65	100635
596 Brady Georg	Schüler	9. 2. 1928	Neustadtl i.M.13	100435
597 Brady Hanna	Schülerin	16. 5. 1931	Neustadtl i.M.13	100436
598 Jillisch Anna	Haushalt	27. 1. 1901	Bzchesstz 28	100714
599 Blum Irene	Haushalt	15.10. 1891	Gr. Meseritsch Jalimilg.20	100493
600 Buchsbaum Elsa	Haushalt	13.12. 1892	Gr. Meseritsch Jalimilg.20	100418

Av

From this list Fumiko learns that Hana had a brother.

There was something else that Fumiko noticed. Beside Hana's name was a tick. In fact, there was a tick beside every name on the page — except one. Beside the other Brady, George Brady, there was nothing. What did this mean?

Theresienstadt, 1943–44

As the days and months passed, Theresienstadt became more crowded and cramped. New trainloads of people arrived all the time. This meant that there was less food for everyone and people became weak and sick. The oldest and youngest people were most at risk.

One day, after she had been in the ghetto for a year, Hana received an urgent message from her brother: Meet me at the Boys' House at six in the evening. I have a wonderful surprise for you.

George couldn't wait to share the good news. "Grandmother is here! She arrived last night!"

The children were overjoyed at the thought of seeing their grandmother. They were also worried. George and Hana's grandmother was a refined woman who had lived a cultured, comfortable life in the capital city of Prague. It was this generous grandmother who had given them their scooters. When they visited her in the big city, she always gave them bananas and oranges. But in recent years, she had been quite ill. How would she manage in this awful place? Not well, it turned out.

PHOTO: KATHY KACER

The now-renovated girls' barracks in Theresienstadt, where Hana lived.

The children found her in an overcrowded attic, with only straw to sleep on, one of many old, sick people. It was the middle of July and the attic was boiling hot. They were horrified by what they saw. Their gentle, elegant grandmother looked terrible. Her beautiful white hair, always so perfectly combed in the past, was a mess. Her clothes were torn and soiled. "I've brought you one of my paintings," Hana exclaimed, thinking it might put a smile on the old woman's face. But her grandmother could barely turn her head. Instead Hana folded the coarse paper and made her painting into a fan. "Rest," she told her grandmother as she tried to create a cooling breeze. Hana felt proud to be in charge of trying to help her grandmother feel better.

Hana soon learned that old people in Theresienstadt were given the smallest and worst rations. The food her grandmother got just wasn't enough and was often crawling with bugs. And there was no medicine. The children visited as often as they could and tried to cheer her up, bringing crafts they'd made and singing songs they'd learned. "This bad time will all be over soon," George told her. "Mother and Father are counting on us all to stay strong," Hana said.

But in three months' time, their grandmother was dead. Beyond Hana and George, few people took much notice. Death was all around them. In fact, so many people were dying so fast, the cemetery was full. Clinging to each other, Hana and George tried to remember the happy times with their grandmother, and cried together.

As more people poured into Terezin, thousands more poured out. They were crammed into frieght trains and sent eastward to an unknown fate. Rumours about the transportations spread inside the walls of Theresienstadt. Some tried to convince themselves and others that a better life awaited the people who were sent away on the trains. But as time went on, stories of death camps, brutality and mass murder circulated widely. When people spoke of these things, Hana covered her ears.

Every few weeks, the dreaded lists would be posted

in each building. People whose names were on them had to report to an assembly hall close to the railway station within two days.

Lists. Everywhere there were lists. The Nazis were systematic record keepers and they wanted all their prisoners to know how they worked. Through the constant counting and listing of people, the Nazis reminded the inmates who was in charge. Everyone knew that being counted, being noticed, could mean a transportation and another separation from family and friends.

One morning, as Hana was doing her chores, everyone in the camp was ordered to stop what they were doing and assemble on a huge field outside the town. Everyone, old and young. They were marched out by Nazi guards carrying machine guns, and ordered to stand there with no food, no water, and a sense that something terrible was about to happen. Hana and the other girls didn't even dare to whisper among themselves.

Hana couldn't bear the thought that she might be separated from George. Or from the girls in Kinderheim L410, who had become almost like sisters. Wasn't it enough that her parents had been taken away from her? Ella stood beside her and tried to cheer her up with smiles and winks. But after four hours of standing, Hana could no longer contain her despair. She began to cry.

Ella slipped her a tiny piece of bread she had hidden in her coat. "Eat this, Hana," she quietly implored. "You will feel better." But Hana's tears kept coming. The big girl then turned to her. "Listen carefully to me," she whispered. "You are unhappy and scared. That's just how the Nazis want to see us, all of us. You can't give them the satisfaction, Hana. You can't give them what they want. We are stronger and better than that. You must dry up those tears, Hana, and put on a brave face." Miraculously, Hana did.

The Nazi commander began shouting out names. Everyone had to be accounted for. Finally, after eight hours of standing in a bitter wind, everyone was ordered to march back to the barracks.

It was September, 1944. When the Nazis began to realise that they were losing the war, they announced that more people would be leaving Theresienstadt. The transports were sped up. Now a new list of names went up every day.

Each morning, her heart pounding, Hana ran down to the main entrance of the building where the list was posted. And one day there it was — the name she dreaded finding — George Brady. Hana's knees buckled. She sat down on the ground and cried. George, her beloved brother, her protector, was being sent away to the east. That wiry boy, now a young man, was told to report to the trains along with 2,000 other able-bodied men.

At their last meeting, on the dirt path between the Boys' House and Kinderheim L410, George asked Hana to listen carefully. "I leave tomorrow," he said. "Now, more than ever, you must eat as much as you can. You must breathe fresh air at every opportunity. You must take care of your health. Be strong. Here is my last ration. Eat every last crumb."

George gave Hana a huge bear hug and gently pushed the hair out of her eyes. "I promised Mother and Father that I would take care of you and bring you home safely so that we can all be together as a family again. I don't want to break that promise." Then the curfew whistle blew and George was gone.

Hana became despondent. She couldn't bear the separation from her brother. First her parents, and now George. She felt so terribly alone in the world. Sometimes, when the other girls tried to cheer her up, Hana turned her face away or even snapped at them, "Can't you just leave me alone?"

Only gentle Ella could convince her to eat her meagre rations. "Remember what your brother told you. You need to take care of yourself and stay strong — for him."

Four weeks later, Hana learned that she, too, was going east. A reunion! "I'll see George again," she told everyone. "He's waiting for me."

She sought out Ella. "Can you help me?" she asked. "I want to look nice when I see my brother. I want to show him how well I've taken care of myself." Despite her own fears, Ella wanted to nourish the hopes of her young friend. She smiled at Hana and set to work. She got water at the pump and used her last little square of soap to wash Hana's face and to clean her knotted, dirty hair. With a piece of rag she tied Hana's hair into a ponytail. She pinched Hana's cheeks to give her a little colour. Ella stood back and looked at the results of her efforts. Hana's face shone with hope. "Thank you Ella," Hana said, hugging the bigger girl. "I don't know what I would do without you." For the first time since George had been sent away, she looked happy.

That night, Hana packed her suitcase. There wasn't much to put into it: a few pieces of pretty worn out clothing, one of her favourite drawings from Friedl's art class, a book of stories that Ella had given her. When she was done, Hana got into her bunk and slept her last night in Theresienstadt.

The next morning, she and many of the other girls from Kinderheim L410 were marched out to the railway track. Nazi guards barked orders and their dogs bared their teeth and growled. No one stepped out of line.

"Where do you think we are going?" Hana whispered to Ella. No one really knew. The girls boarded the darkened freight wagon one by one, until there was not an inch of room left in the train. The air turned sour. And the wheels began to turn.

The train chugged on for a day and a night. There was no food. There was no water. There was no toilet. The girls had no idea how long the journey would be. Their throats were parched, their bones ached, their stomachs rumbled with hunger.

They tried to comfort each other, singing songs of home. "Lean on me," Ella said softly, "and listen, Hana."

So when I want to cry the blues
I just recall the centipede.
Consider walking in her shoes
And then my life seems sweet indeed.

The girls held hands. They closed their eyes and tried to imagine being somewhere else. Each girl imagined something different. When Hana closed her eyes, she saw the strong, smiling face of her brother.

And then suddenly, in the middle of the night on 23 October, 1944, the wheels of the train ground to a screeching halt. The doors were opened. The girls were ordered out of the freight wagon. This was Auschwitz.

An angry guard ordered them to stand straight and silent on the platform. He held tight the leash of a large dog straining to pounce. The guard looked the group up and down quickly. He cracked his whip in the direction of one girl who had always been embarrassed by how tall she was. "You," he said, "over there, to the right!" He cracked his whip one more time at another of the older girls. "You, there too." Then he called over to a group of young soldiers who stood at the edge of the platform. "Take them, now!" he ordered, pointing to Hana and the rest of her group. Huge searchlights almost blinded the girls. "Leave your suitcases on the platform," the soldiers commanded.

Through a wrought iron gate and under the watchful eyes of the surly dogs and uniformed men, Hana and her old roommates were marched off. Hana held on tightly to Ella's hand. They passed huge barracks, saw the skeleton-like faces of prisoners in their striped uniforms peeking out the doors. They were ordered to enter a large building. The door closed behind them with a frightening bang.

Terezin, July 2000

"What does the tick mean?" asked Fumiko, as she looked at the page listing Hana Brady and George Brady.

Ludmila hesitated and then spoke carefully. "The tick means that the person didn't survive."

Fumiko lowered her eyes to the paper again. Hana's name had a tick beside it. Like almost all the 15,000 children who passed through Theresienstadt, Hana had died at Auschwitz.

Fumiko bowed her head and closed her eyes. She had already guessed the awful truth. But hearing it spoken, seeing it on paper was still a blow. Fumiko sat silently for a few minutes, trying to take it all in.

And then she gathered herself together and looked up. Hana's story was not over. Now, more than ever, Fumiko wanted to know everything about her — for herself, for the children waiting for her back in Japan, and for Hana's memory. She absolutely determined that this life, ended so unjustly, at such a young age, would not be forgotten. It had become her mission to make sure of this. The quest was not over.

"There is no tick beside George's name," Fumiko

said. "Is there any way," she stammered, "that we can find out about him? What happened to him? Where did he go? Is he still alive?" If she could only find him, he might help her discover more about Hana. Fumiko began to tremble with excitement.

Ludmila looked sadly across the desk at Fumiko. She could see how badly Fumiko wanted to know. "I have no idea what happened to him," she said softly. "The war was such a long time ago, you know. He could have gone anywhere in the world. He could even have changed his name. Or he could have died, long after the war."

"Please," Fumiko pleaded, "you have to help me find him."

The woman sighed and turned back to the bookshelves crammed with bound volumes of names on lists. "We can keep looking for clues in here," she said. For an hour, Fumiko and Ludmila sorted through books filled with names, looking for another mention of George Brady. And finally, they found one.

He was on the list of inmates of Kinderheim L417, the Boys' House at Theresienstadt. The names were clumped in groups of six, since two boys shared each mattress in the three-tiered bunks. When Ludmila checked the names listed with George Brady, she looked up at Fumiko with a start.

"Kurt Kotouc," she said. "Kurt Kotouc," she repeated. "I know that name. He's alive. I think George

Brady's bunkmate used to live in Prague, but I have no idea where. If we can locate him, maybe he can tell you what happened to Hana's brother. Unfortunately, there's nothing more I can do for you here. Try the Jewish Museum in Prague. Maybe someone there can help."

Fumiko thanked Ludmila over and over again for all she had done. She hugged her and promised to let her know about the results of her detective work. Ludmila wished Fumiko luck. Then Fumiko picked up her briefcase and ran out of the office into the town square. The bus for Prague was due at any moment.

Prague, July 2000

Fumiko had only a few hours of daytime left before her plane left for Japan early the next morning. As soon as she got off the bus in Prague, she hailed a taxi. "The Jewish Museum, please," she said, trying to catch her breath.

She arrived at the Prague Jewish Museum just before closing time. The guard told her to come back the next day. "But I can't," pleaded Fumiko. "I have to go back to Japan tomorrow morning. I'm here to see Michaela Hajek. She helped me find some very important drawings." When nothing else seemed to convince the guard, Fumiko bent the truth a little. "She's expecting me," Fumiko told the man confidently. And he let her in.

This time, luck was on Fumiko's side. The woman was in her office and remembered the story of Hana. She listened carefully as Fumiko explained what she had found out.

"I have heard of Kurt Kotouc," Michaela said quietly. Fumiko could barely believe it. "I will try and help you find him," Michaela promised. She understood that Fumiko had no time to lose.

Fumiko sat quietly as Michaela made phone call after phone call. Each person Michaela spoke to gave her another number to try and wished her well in the search. Finally she reached an office where Mr. Kotouc worked as an art historian. She handed the phone to Fumiko who tried to explain what she was looking for. The secretary wanted to help, but told her Mr. Kotouc was leaving on an overseas trip that evening. "I'm sorry," she said to Fumiko, "a meeting will be impossible." No, he didn't even have time for a phone call.

Michaela watched as Fumiko's face fell. She got back on the phone herself and pleaded with the secretary. "You have no idea how desperate this young woman is. She has to go back to Japan in the morning. This is her only chance." The secretary finally relented.

Two hours later, the sky was dark and the Museum was officially closed. All the staff had gone home. But one office was still brightly lit. There, Fumiko and Michaela awaited the arrival of Mr. Kotouc.

Finally he came. The heavyset man with bright eyes had much to tell. "I only have half an hour," he said, "before I leave for the airport. Of course, I remember George Brady. We shared a bunk in Theresienstadt and much more. You never forget the connections you make with people in a place like Theresienstadt. Not only that," he said, "we are still friends. He lives in Toronto, Canada."

Mr. Kotouc pulled out a small leather book. "Here's what you're looking for," he said with a smile.

He wrote down George Brady's address and gave it to Fumiko. "Oh, Mr. Kotouc, I can't thank you enough," Fumiko said.

"Good luck," he told Fumiko. "I'm so happy that children in Japan want to understand the lessons of the Holocaust." And then Mr. Kotouc dashed out of the office, baggage in hand.

Fumiko beamed from ear to ear. All her persistence had paid off. She told Michaela how grateful she was for her help.

The next morning Fumiko settled in her seat for the long flight to Japan. She was still tingling with excitement. She tried to recall all the news she had for the children at the Centre. When she thought about Hana having a big brother, Fumiko couldn't help picturing her own little sister, three years younger. Fumiko had always looked after her and she tried to imagine what she would do if her little sister were in danger. The very thought made her shudder. She looked out the window as the story repeated itself over and over in her mind. After an hour, she fell into a deep sleep, the first one she'd had in a long time.

Tokyo, August 2000

Back in Tokyo, Fumiko called a special meeting of Small Wings. She shared every detail of her adventure with the members. The sad news came first. With the children around her in a circle, Fumiko told them, in a quiet voice, what they had already imagined. Hana had died at Auschwitz.

"But I have a wonderful surprise," Fumiko said. The faces of the children brightened. "Hana had a brother named George — and he survived!"

The questions started flying at once. "Where is he?" asked Maiko. "How old is he?" one boy wanted to know. "Does he know that we have Hana's suitcase?" asked Akira. Fumiko told them everything she knew. And she said she would work late that very night so that she could write George a letter.

"Can we send something with it?" asked Maiko. The older children scattered to quiet spots around the Centre to compose poems. "What can I do?" Akira asked Maiko.

"Draw a picture of Hana," she replied.

"But I don't know what she looks like," he said.

"Just draw her as you imagine her," Maiko said.

A tribute to Hana by children at the Holocaust Centre.
They used the German spelling of Hana's name because it
was spelled that way on the suitcase.

And Akira did.

Fumiko wrote her own letter very carefully. She knew that receiving it would come as a shock to George. She knew that some Holocaust survivors refused to ever speak about their experiences. She worried that his memories might be so bitter and painful that he wouldn't want to hear anything about Hana's suitcase and the Holocaust Centre in Japan.

Fumiko had copies made of Hana's drawings and packaged them carefully, along with the children's writings and artwork. Then she took the parcel down to the post office, crossed her fingers, and sent it off to Canada.

Toronto, Canada
August 2000

It was a warm and sunny August afternoon. Seventy-two-year-old George Brady had come home from work early and had planned to spend a quiet afternoon at home, sorting out some bills. He was sitting at his dining room table when he heard the footsteps of the postman, the whoosh of envelopes being shoved through the letterbox, and the thump of them landing on the floor. I'll get them later, he thought. Then the doorbell rang.

When he opened the door, the postman was standing there. "This wouldn't fit through," he said, handing a package to George. The package was postmarked Japan. What could this be? George wondered. He didn't know anyone in Japan.

When he opened the package and began to read the letter, George's heart began to pound. He closed his eyes. He opened them, blinking hard, making sure that what he was reading was real. Was this a daydream he was having?

The loss of his sister Hana was George's most private and deepest sorrow. He had lived with it for over half a century and had never been able to get over

George Brady today.

the feeling that he should have been able to protect his little sister.

Now, somehow, halfway around the world, her story was being told and her life was being honoured. George was stunned. He sat down and let his mind wander back fifty-five years.

When Auschwitz was liberated in January 1945, George Brady was seventeen years old. He had survived the horrors of the camp by starting out young and strong, by good luck, and by using the trade he had learned at Theresienstadt — plumbing. When he was freed, he was very weak and painfully thin. But George was determined to make his way back to Nove Mesto

ホロコースト教育資料センター
Tokyo Holocaust Education Resource Center

~*For Children, Builders of Peace*

〒160-0015 東京都新宿区大京町28-105
TEL:03-5363-4808 FAX:03-5363-4809

28-105 Daikyo-cho,Shinjuku-ku Tokyo,160-0015 JAPAN
TEL:+81-3-5363-4808 FAX:+81-3-5363-4809
E-mail : Holocaust@Tokyo.email.ne.jp
Homepage : http://www.ne.jp/asahi/holocaust/tokyo

Mr. George Brady
23 Blyth Hill Road
Toronto 12, M4N 3L5
CANADA

August 22, 2000

Dear Mr. Brady,

We take a liberty of addressing and telling you about our activities in Japan. My name is Fumiko Ishioka and I am Director of Tokyo Holocaust Education Resource Center. In July this year I met with Mr. Kurt Jiri Kotouc in Prague and I got your address from him. The reason why I am writing to you is because we are now exhibiting your sister, Hanna Brady's suitcase at our Center. Please forgive me if my letter hurts you reminding you of your past difficult experiences. But I would very much appreciate it if you could kindly spare some time to read this letter.

Please let me start with a little explanation on what we do in Japan. Tokyo Holocaust Education Resource Center, established in October 1998, is a non-profit, educational organization that aims at further promoting understanding of the history of the Holocaust especially among young children in this country. Children here do not have a chance to learn about the Holocaust, but we believe it is our responsibility too to let our next generation learn the lessons of the Holocaust so that such a tragedy would never be repeated again anywhere in the world. As well as learning the truth of the Holocaust, it is also very important for children, we believe, to think about what they can do to fight against racism and intolerance and to create peace by their own hands.

Besides welcoming children at our Center for exhibition and study programs, this year we organized a pair of traveling exhibition, "The Holocaust Seen Through Children's Eyes" in order to reach more children living far from our Center. For this project, we borrowed some children's memorial items from individuals and museums in Europe, one of which is Hanna Brady's suitcase from the museum of Auschwitz. Many children are now visiting our Center to see this suitcase to learn about the Holocaust. In June, furthermore, we held the Children's Forum on the Holocaust 2000, where our Center's children's group "Small Wings" did a little opening performance on Hanna's suitcase. "Small Wings" is a group of children, aged from 8 to 18, who write newsletters and make videos to let their friends know about the Holocaust and share what they learn from it. At the Forum they decided to use Hanna's suitcase to do an introduction for their friends who have never heard of the Holocaust. It successfully helped participants of the Forum focus on one little life, among one and a half million, lost during the Holocaust, and think about importance of remembering this history.

When I received the suitcase from the museum of Auschwitz, all the information I had were things written on the suitcase, her name and her birthday, and from the Terezin memorial book I got the date when she was deported to Auschwitz. I could also find 4 of her drawings from Terezin. But that was all. Hoping to get more information on Hanna, I went to Terezin in July, when I found your name on the list I got from the ghetto museum and heard that you survived. I was then so lucky to find Mr.Kotouc in Prague and met with him, from whom I heard you now live in Toronto. Those children of "Small Wings" were all so excited to know Hanna had a brother and he survived.

I was wondering if you would kindly be able to tell us about you and Hanna's story, the time you spent with Hanna before sent to the camp, things that you talked with her, you and her dreams, and anything that would help children here feel close to you and Hanna to understand what prejudice, intolerance and hatred did to young Jewish children. If possible, I would be grateful if you could lent us any kind of memorial items such as your family's photo, and so on. It will greatly help us further promote our goal to give every child in Japan a chance to learn about the Holocaust.

Thank you very much for your time. I would very much appreciate your kind understanding for our activities.

I look forward to hearing from you.

With kindest regards,

Fumiko Ishioka
Director
Tokyo Holocaust Education Resource Center

Fumiko's letter to George.

— to his parents and his little sister Hana. He desperately wanted his family to be together again.

By foot, by train and by hitchhiking, George made it back to the home he loved in May 1945. He went straight for Uncle Ludvik and Aunt Hedda's house. It was the last place where he had known family, love and safety. When they opened the door and found their nephew standing there, aunt and uncle fell on him — hugging, kissing, touching, crying — barely able to believe that George was alive.

But the unbridled happiness of the reunion was short-lived. "Where are Mother and Father?" George asked. Ludvik and Hedda were forced to tell him the terrible truth. Marketa had been sent from Ravensbruck to Auschwitz and murdered there in 1942. Karel was killed there the same year. "And Hana?" George whispered. All his aunt and uncle knew was that she had been sent to Auschwitz.

For months, George nursed the faint hope that somehow, somewhere, Hana would appear. He searched for her in every young girl's face he saw, in every ponytail that swished by, in every jaunty step of a healthy child on the street. One day, George encountered a teenage girl on the main street in Prague. She stopped in front of him.

"George?" she asked. "Are you not George Brady, Hana's brother? My name is Marta. I knew Hana. All of us older girls at Theresienstadt loved her." George searched Marta's eyes for information, for hope. She realized that George didn't yet know the final truth about his sister. "George," she told him quietly, plainly, taking hold of his hands. "Hana was sent to be killed in the gas chamber at Auschwitz, the same day she arrived there. I'm sorry, George. Hana is dead." George's knees turned to jelly and the world went black.

Toronto,
August 2000

In the more than half a century since George learned the terrible fates of his parents and sister, much had happened. At seventeen, George had left Nove Mesto. He moved from city to city in Europe, carrying his only treasured possession — the box of family photographs that Uncle Ludvik and Aunt Hedda had hidden for him. Then, in early 1951, he moved to Toronto and set up a plumbing business with another Holocaust survivor. It was very successful. George married, became the father of three sons and, much later, of a daughter.

George was proud of the fact that — despite his suffering during the Holocaust and the fact that his mother, father and sister had been murdered by the Nazis — he had moved on with his life. He was a successful businessman, a proud father. He thought of himself as a healthy person who, for the most part, put his wartime experiences behind him. But whatever he accomplished, whatever joy he felt, it was always tinged with the memory of his beautiful little sister and the horror of her fate.

And now, here he was, with a letter from halfway around the world, telling him how his sister's suitcase was helping a new generation of Japanese children learn about the Holocaust. The letter from Fumiko also asked, very gently, for his help.

Please forgive me, if my letter hurts you by reminding you of your difficult experiences. But I would very much appreciate if you would kindly be able to tell us about your and Hana's story. We would like to know about the time you spent with Hana before you were sent to the camp, the things that you talked with her about, your and her dreams. We are interested in anything that would help children here in Japan feel close to you and Hana. We want to understand what prejudice, intolerance, and hatred did to young Jewish children.

If possible, I would also be grateful if you could lend us any family photos. I know that most Holocaust survivors lost their family photographs, along with their families. But if you do have any pictures, it would greatly help us with our goal to give every child in Japan a chance to learn about the Holocaust. We at the Tokyo Holocaust Centre and the children of Small Wings are all so excited to know that Hana had a brother and that he survived.

It was signed "Fumiko Ishioka".

George could hardly believe it. Such amazing connections and strange coincidences had brought three worlds together: the world of children in Japan, George in Canada, and the lost world of a Jewish girl from Czechoslovakia who died so long ago. George wiped the tears from his cheek and then smiled to himself. Hana's young face was so clear to him. He could almost hear her laugh, and feel her soft hand in his. George went to the large wooden dresser and pulled out a photograph album. He wanted to get in touch with Fumiko Ishioka as soon as possible.

Tokyo,
September 2000

Ever since she had sent the letter to Toronto, Fumiko had been a bundle of nerves. Would George Brady write back? Would he help us to know Hana? Even the postman who delivered the post to the Centre knew how anxious Fumiko was. "Anything from Canada today?" she would ask the minute she saw him walking up the path to the front door. He hated to see her disappointment when, day after day, the answer was no.

Then, on the last day of the month, Fumiko was in the middle of welcoming forty guests to the Centre. They were teachers and students who had come to learn about the Holocaust and to see the suitcase. Out of the corner of her eye, through a window, she saw the postman walking very quickly toward the building with a huge smile on his face. Fumiko excused herself and ran to meet him. "Here it is," he said, beaming. And he handed her a thick envelope from Toronto.

Fumiko screamed. She couldn't help it. Some of the visiting teachers and students rushed to her office door. "What's wrong? What's the matter?" they asked.

"Nothing is wrong," she told them, stumbling over

Hana.

her words. "I'm just so happy, so excited. Here, look, this is a picture of Hana. This is the beautiful little girl whose story we have worked so hard to find."

Along with the photographs, there was a long letter from George. In it, Fumiko learned about Hana's happy early days in Nove Mesto, about her family, and how she loved to ski and skate. It was comforting to know that Hana had had a good life before the war ruined everything.

And Fumiko learned about George, too. As she read about his life in Canada, his children and his grandchildren, Fumiko was bursting with happiness. She began to cry. He survived, she repeated over and over to herself. He survived. More than that, he has a beautiful family. She couldn't wait to tell the children of Small Wings.

Tokyo,
March 2001

"Calm down," Fumiko said with a smile. "They'll be here soon, I promise."

But nothing she said could tame the excitement of the children that morning. They buzzed around the Centre, checked their poems, straightened their clothes for the umpteenth time, told silly jokes just to make the time move faster. Even Maiko, whose job it was to calm everyone else down, was jumpy.

Then, finally, the waiting was over. George Brady had arrived. And he had brought with him his seventeen-year-old daughter, Lara Hana.

Now the children became very quiet. At the Centre's front entrance, they crowded around George. They bowed to him, as is the custom in Japan. George bowed back. Akira presented George with a beautiful multi-coloured origami garland. All the children jostled gently for the chance to be nearest to him. After so many months of hearing about George from Fumiko, they were thrilled to finally meet him in person.

Fumiko took George's arm. "Come with us, now, and see your sister's suitcase." They walked to the display area.

Fumiko holds a picture of the suitcase as George Brady talks to children during his trip to Japan and the Holocaust Centre.

And there, surrounded by the children, with Fumiko holding one of his hands and his daughter, Lara, holding the other, George saw the suitcase for the first time in over half a century.

Suddenly, an almost unbearable sadness came over him. Here was the suitcase that belonged to his little sister. There was her name written right on it. Hana Brady. His beautiful, strong, mischievous, generous, fun-loving sister. She had died so young and in such a terrible way. George lowered his head and let the tears flow freely.

But, a few minutes later, when he looked up, he saw his daughter. He saw Fumiko, who had worked so hard to find him and the story of Hana. And he saw the expectant faces of all those Japanese children for whom Hana had become so important, so alive.

George realised that, in the end, one of Hana's wishes had come true. Hana had become a teacher. Because of her — her suitcase and her story — thousands of Japanese children were learning about what George believed to be the most important values in the world: tolerance, respect and compassion. What a gift Fumiko and the children have given me, he thought. And what an honour they have given Hana.

Fumiko asked the children to sit in a circle. She beamed with pride as, one by one, they presented George with their drawings and poems about Hana. When they had finished, Maiko stood up, took a deep breath, and read a poem aloud.

Hana Brady, thirteen years old, was the owner of this suitcase.
Fifty-five years ago, 18 May, 1942 — two days after Hana's eleventh birthday — she was taken to Terezin in Czechoslovakia.
23 October, 1944, crowded into the freight train, she was sent to Auschwitz.
She was taken to the gas chamber right after.
People were allowed to take only one suitcase with them.
I wonder what Hana put in her suitcase.

Hana would have been sixty-nine years old today, but her life stopped when she was thirteen.

I wonder what kind of girl she was.

A few drawings she made at Terezin — these are the only things she left for us.

What do these drawings tell us?

Happy memories of her family?

Dreams and hopes for the future?

Why was she killed?

There was one reason.

She was born Jewish.

Name: Hana Brady. Date of Birth: 16 May, 1931. Orphan.

We, Small Wings, will tell every child in Japan what happened to Hana.

We, Small Wings, will never forget what happened to one-and-a-half-million Jewish children.

We children can make a difference in building peace in the world — so that the Holocaust will never happen again.

By Small Wings, December 2000, Tokyo, Japan.
Translated from Japanese by Fumiko Ishioka.

While Maiko reads on the left, members of the Small Wings hold up signs saying 'Let's Learn, Think and Act [to create peace] for the 21st century'.

Postscript

Hana's suitcase continues its journey.

After spending time with the children at the Holocaust Centre in Tokyo, George and Lara Brady, along with Fumiko Ishioka and Small Wings leader Maiko Kurihara, visited Hiroshima to share Hana's story with students and teachers there.

As of May 2002, the exhibition 'The Holocaust Seen Through Children's Eyes' has travelled to over fifty places around Japan, and has been seen by more than 52,000 people.

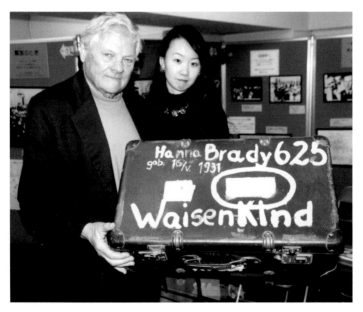

Acknowledgements

First and foremost, my thanks go to George Brady and Fumiko Ishioka. This is their story. Each of them, with remarkable dedication and generosity, helped to bring the book together. They are very tenacious and compassionate people, driven by the desire to make the world a better place, and to bring attention and honour to the memory of Hana Brady. I salute them.

My heart jumped the first time I learned of Hana's suitcase in an article by Paul Lungen in the *Canadian Jewish News*. The story so touched me that I decided to come out of "exile" and produce my first radio documentary in a dozen years. The result was "Hana's Suitcase," which aired on *The Sunday Edition* on CBC Radio One in January 2001.

The first phone call I received after the broadcast came from a tearful Margie Wolfe, who said right then and there that I had to write this book. Margie is one of my favourite people in the whole world — a fiercely loyal friend, and a hilarious, kooky, exuberantly talented woman whom I can now refer to as "my publisher" with feigned nonchalance.

Along with Margie, Sarah Swartz brought a clear and gentle touch to the editorial process. Jeffrey Canton, as well as the women of Second Story Press,

Carolyn Foster and Laura McCurdy, also made important contributions. Reynold Gonsalves knows that without his patience and skill in the radio studio and on the computer, my life would be much more complicated than it already is. Thank you also to Carmelita Tenerife for her sustaining care and Teresa Brady for her kindness.

My sensational circle of women friends were morale boosters, babysitters, and all-round hand holders in this writing project: Susanne Boyce, Cate Cochran, Joy Crysdale, Brooke Forbes, Francine Pelletier, Geraldine Sherman and Talin Vartanian. I want to give special thanks to 9-year-old Madeline Cochran for being an early reader of the manuscript. Her (and her mother's) suggestions were great!

No daughter could ask for more support and cheerleading from her parents. My mother, Helen, and my father, Gil, taught me (among many other things) to celebrate human struggle, to know the past and to fight for a better future. And they gave me the best big sister, Ruthie Tamara, who has encouraged me in every way.

Michael Enright — my beau and co-vivant — thought I could write a book long before I did, and never missed an opportunity to tell me so. His confidence in me, and his unvarnished enthusiasm about this project, terrified and thrilled me at the same time. At every step, he gave me the nourishment I wanted, the prodding I needed and the room to work. I am truly grateful for it all. I am also grateful for the true-heartedness of the Enright brood — Daniel, Anthony and Nancy.

My son — Gabriel Zev Enright Levine — is six years old now, too young to know Hana's story. But when he is old enough, I'll read it to him. I hope he will be as drawn to Hana, George and Fumiko as I was. I also hope he will learn from the story that history matters, and that despite the most unspeakable evil, good people and good deeds can make a difference.